Tools

OF THE

Greater Key

AUTHOR'S NOTE: Text in italics is taken from *The Goetia: The Lesser Key of
Solomon the King (Clavicula Salomonis Regis)* and *The Key of Solomon the King
(Clavicula Salomonis)*. I have left this text as it stands so that people can
infer what they will from the description of the tools' usage.

TOOLS

OF THE

GREATER KEY

S. ALDARNAY

TABLE OF CONTENTS

INTRODUCTION

THE *GREATER KEY OF SOLOMON* IS ARGUABLY ONE OF THE MOST INFLUENTIAL grimoires in modern magical practice; however, like so many of the older books of magic, over the years many of the images, symbols, and sigils found in the book have become distorted and malformed by time and human error. In this volume I have endeavoured to render the images found in the popular Mathers edition of the text clearly and cleanly, so that they might be of greater use to the modern magician, either as physical tools, or as a way of understanding the symbolic and ritualistic virtues of the objects contained within this famous magical text.

The tools of the *Greater Key* are a useful addition to the magical arsenal of many modern practitioners, and with this book I aim to provide simple blueprints the reader can use to create their own tools using the images and commentary provided. As well as the tools from the *Greater Key of Solomon*, I have also included some of the more practical tools, objects, and diagrams from *Ars Goetia* (the *Lesser Key*) which, whilst having very specific roles within the rites of evocation, may prove of more general use to the inventive magician.

It is worth mentioning from the outset that the exact physical shape of the tools in the Solomonic texts vary greatly between editions, and as such if you do endeavour to produce your own versions of these tools, it is seemingly more important that you maintain the integrity of the symbols and names over the exact shape of the weapon as it is presented.

I have tried to keep the text as presented in Mathers' edition of the *Greater Key* as unchanged as possible, so people can draw their own interpretations from the text, and where changes have been made, I have tried to limit this to places where it was necessary to make the text readable in the context of individual tools. Where I have volunteered my own thoughts on various subjects, I have made sure to keep these entirely separate from the body of the original text, which is both quoted and italicised.

THE PREPARATORY TOOLS

THE FOLLOWING TOOLS ARE USED IN THE PRODUCTION OF OTHER ITEMS, OR as stand-alone pieces of magical kit used in the pre-ritual preparatory process. These include items such as the pens used to write out seals, vessels for manufacturing parchment and the candles used to illuminate the magic circle. I have also included the designs for the circle here, as this text alludes in several places that this should already have been drawn out prior to its consecration.

On the whole, these are practical tools which are used for the more mundane tasks the magician must undertake before the magical act itself can take place. These tools place the magical act more firmly in the physical world, and the level of detail given to items such as the burin and the inkstands, as well as the solemn nature of their consecration, show the way in which from the very outset of even the simplest magical act, every detail must be taken into account and conducted as perfectly as possible. Whilst it may be in the natural reaction of many modern magicians to rush straight into the creation of magical weapons or talismans, it is evident from the text that before these more well-known tools are produced these very basic needs must be met.

I have tried to present each of the tools in a clear fashion so that the signs, names and symbols can be clearly read and copied without distortion, and as with the other chapters of this book, the tools are not arranged in any specific fashion; however, I would recommend that the pens and the burin are the most useful tools to create first, as most of the other tools require them in their composition.

A Convenient Circle

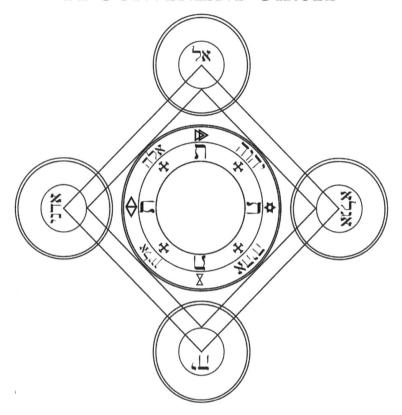

This circle is given at the very start of the Mathers edition of the *Key*, described simply as "*A convenient form of circle which may be used for preparing instruments and other things of the same kind.*"

It is similar to the other circle given in the text, but is somewhat simpler; it lacks the additional square and subsequently reduces the number of censers required from 8 to 4. There are no descriptions for the creation or consecration of this circle; however, methods can be extrapolated from the other entry on circles found later in the text.

Censers are to be placed in the 4 small circles at the points of the square – presumably placed over the divine names. In the diagram I have provided, the topmost point of the circle (that which contains the divine name EL) points towards the east.

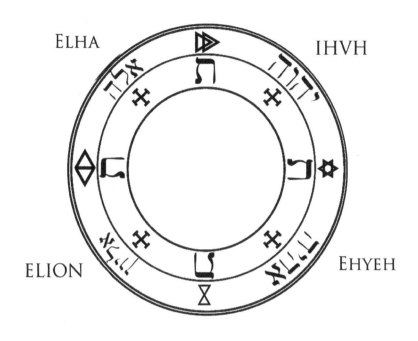

ELHA

IHVH

ELION

EHYEH

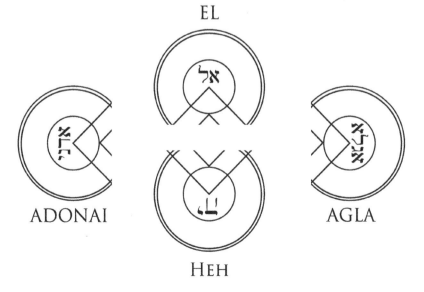

EL

ADONAI

AGLA

HEH

THE BURIN

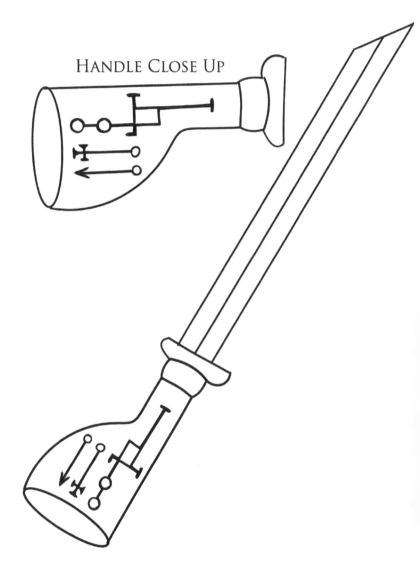

There are several steel instruments necessary in various operations, as a needle to pierce or to sew: a burin, or instrument wherewith to engrave...

"Thou shalt make such instruments in the day and hour of Jupiter, and when it is finished thou shalt say:

"I conjure thee, O instrument of steel, by God The Father Almighty, by the virtue of the heavens, of the stars, and of the angels who preside over them; by the virtue of stones, herbs and animals; by the virtue of hail, snow and wind, that thou receives such virtue that thou mayest obtain without deceit the end which I desire in all things wherein I shall use thee; through God the Creator of the Ages, and Emperor of the Angels. Amen.

"Afterwards repeat Psalms III, IX, XXXI, XLII, LX, LI, CXXX (3, 9, 31, 42, 60, 51 & 130).

"Perfume it with the perfumes of the art and sprinkle it with exorcised water, wrap it in silk and say:

"Dani, Zumech, Agalmaturod, Gadiel, Pani, Caneloas, Merod, Gamidoi, Baldoi, Metrator, Angels Most Holy, be present for a guard unto this instrument."

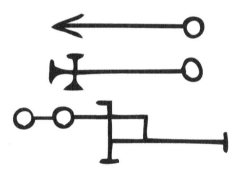

Burins can be purchased cheaply from art and craft supplies shops and usually have a wooden handle which will easily take the requisite symbols.

The Candles

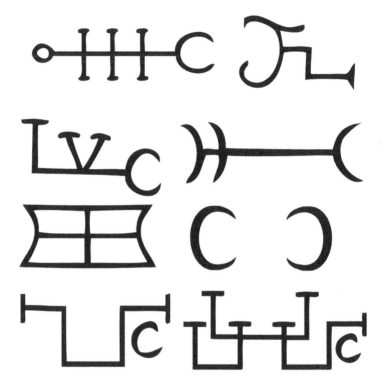

"It hath been ever the custom among all nations to use fire and light in sacred things. For this reason the Master of the Art should also employ them in sacred rites, and besides those for reading the Conjurations by, and for the incense, in all operations Lights are necessary in the Circle.

"For this reason he should make candles of virgin wax in the day and hour of Mercury; the wicks should have been made by a young girl; and the Candles should be made when the moon is in her increase, of the weight of half a pound each, and on them thou shalt engrave these characters with the Dagger, or the Burin of Art.

"After this thou shalt repeat over the Candles, Psalms CLI.; CIII.; CVII (151,

103, 107), and shalt say:

"O Lord God, Who governest all things by Thine Almighty Power, give unto me, a poor sinner, understanding and knowledge to do only that which is agreeable unto Thee; grant unto me to fear, adore, love, praise, and give thanks unto Thee with true and sincere faith and perfect charity. Grant, O Lord, before I die, and descend into the realms beneath, and before the fiery flame shall devour me, that Thy Grace may not leave me, O Lord of my Soul. Amen.

"After this thou shalt add:
"I exorcise thee, O Creature of wax, by Him Who alone hath created all things by His Word, and by the virtue of Him Who is pure truth, that thou cast out from thee every Phantasm, Perversion, and Deceit of the Enemy, and may the Virtue and Power of God enter into thee, so that thou mayest give us light, and chase far from us all fear or terror.

"After this thou shalt sprinkle them with the Water of the Art, and incense them with the usual perfumes.

"And when thou shalt wish to kindle them thou shalt say:
"I exorcise thee, O Creature of Fire, in the Name of the Sovereign and Eternal Lord, by His Ineffable Name, which is YOD, HE, VAU, HE; by the Name IAH; and by the Name of Power EL; that thou mayest enlighten the heart of all the Spirits which we shall call unto this Circle, so that they may appear before us without fraud and deceit through Him Who hath created all things.

"Then thou shalt take a square Lantern, with panes of Crystal glass, and thou shalt fit therein the Candle lighted, to read by, to form the Circle, or any other purpose for which thou shalt require."

As you can see above, the candles should be half a pound of wax (approximately 227 grams), which would produce candles akin to dinner tapers, or shorter, squatter, church candles. These may seem fairly small or unimpressive; however, bear in mind the often-quoted caution not to entertain spirits for longer than one hour.

There are other references in the text to lanterns to contain the candles; presumably this shows that the person/people who wrote the original were in fact working outside, as per the instructions in the grimoires. That said, there are no specific instructions for creating such lanterns, or any signs or symbols that should be placed upon them.

THE CIRCLE

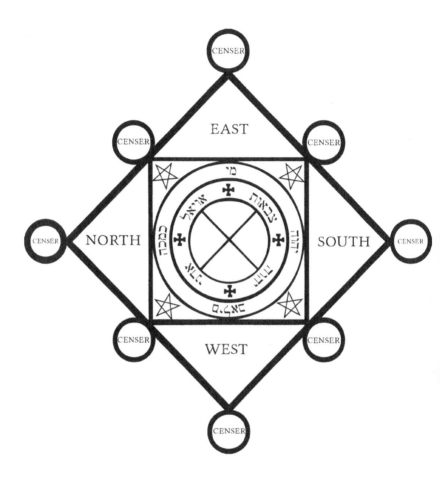

"*Having chosen a place for preparing and constructing the Circle, and al*
things necessary being prepared for the perfection of the Operations, take thou
the Sickle or Scimitar of Art and stick it into the centre of the place where the
Circle is to be made; then take a cord of nine feet in length, fasten one end thereo
unto the Sickle and with the other end trace out the circumference of the Circle
which may be marked either with the Sword or with the Knife with the Black hilt

Then within the Circle mark out four regions, namely, towards the East, West, South, and North, wherein place Symbols; and beyond the limits of this Circle describe with the Consecrated Knife or Sword another Circle, but leaving an open space therein towards the North whereby thou mayest enter and depart beyond the Circle of Art. Beyond this again thou shalt describe another Circle at a foot distance with the aforesaid Instrument, yet ever leaving therein an open space for entrance and egress corresponding to the open space already left in the other. Beyond this again make another Circle at another foot distance, and beyond these two Circles, which are beyond the Circle of Art yet upon the same Centre, thou shalt describe Pentagrams with the Symbols and Names of the Creator therein so that they may surround the Circle already described. Without these Circles shalt thou circumscribe a Square, and beyond that another Square, so that the Angles of the former may touch the centres of the sides of the latter, and that the Angles of the latter may stretch towards the four quarters of the Universe, East, West, North, and South; and at the four Angles of each square, and touching them, thou shalt describe lesser Circles wherein let there be placed standing censers with lighted charcoal and sweet odours.

"These things being done, let the Magus of Art assemble his Disciples, exhort, confirm, and cheer them; lead them into the Circle of Art and station them therein towards the Four Quarters of the Universe, exhort them to fear nothing, and to abide in their assigned places. Furthermore, let each of the Companions have a Sword besides the Sword of the Art, which he must hold naked in his hand. Then let the Magus quit the Circle, and Kindle the Censers, and place thereon exorcised Incense, as is said in the Chapter of Fumigations; and let him have the Censer in his hand and kindle it, and then place it in the part prepared. Let him now enter within the Circle and carefully close the openings left in the same, and let him again warn his Disciples, and take the Trumpet of Art prepared as is said in the Chapter concerning the same, and let him incense the Circle towards the Four Quarters of the Universe.

"After this let the Magus commence his Incantations, having placed the Sickle, Sword, or other Implement of Art upright in the ground at his feet. Having sounded the trumpet as before taught let him invoke the Spirits, and if need be conjure them, as is said in the First Book, and having attained his desired effect, let him license them to depart."

CLOSE-UP OF THE CENTRE OF THE CIRCLE:

NAMES FOUND IN THE OUTER CIRCLE:

צבאות
TZABAOTH

אויאל
AUIEL (?)

אדני
ADONAI

יהוה
IHVI

NAMES FOUND IN THE INNER CIRCLE:

יהוה

IHVH

כמכה

KAMKAH?

באלים

BALIM

מי

MI?

The illustration given in the Mathers edition of the *Key* does not marry up completely with the description given in the text, which instructs for an opening to be created through which the magician may enter and exit without compromising the integrity of the circle. Other editions of the text also show this opening "barred" by a curved weapon (most likely the scimitar or sickle) pointing outwards, away from the magician. It can be assumed that the divine names/signs inscribed on the blade of the weapon will serve in place of those which are removed due to the creation of the exit/entrance.

THE INKSTAND

יהוה : מטטרון :

יה יה יה : קדוש :

אלהים : צבאות :

"*Thou shalt have an inkstand made of earth or any convenient matter, an*
in the day and hour of Mercury, thou shalt engrave thereon with the burin of ar
these names: YOD HE VAU HE, METATRON, IAH IAH IAH, QADOSCH
ELOHIM, TZABAOTH, and in putting the ink therein thou shalt say:

"*I Exorcise thee, O creature of Ink, by ANAIRETON, by SIMULATOR*
and by the name ADONAI, and by the name of him through whom all thing
were made, that thou be unto me and aid in succour in all things which I wish t
perform thine aid."

ENGLISH TRANSLATION OF DIVINE NAMES:

יה יה יה	מטטרון	יהוה
IAH IAH IAH	METATRON	IHVH

צבאות	אלהים	קדוש
TZABAOTH	ELOHIM	QADOSCH

THE PEN OF THE SWALLOW AND THE CROW

"Take the feather of a Swallow or of a Crow, and before plucking it thou shalt say:

"May Holy MICHAEL the Archangel of God, and MIDAEL and MIRAEL, the Chiefs and Captains of the Celestial Army, be my aid in the operation I am about to perform, so that I may write herewith all things which are necessary, and that all the experiments which I commence herewith may through you and through your Names be perfected by the power of the Most High Creator. Amen.

"After this thou shalt point and complete the pen with the Knife of the Art, and with the pen and ink of the Art thou shalt write upon its side the Name, ANAIRETON, and thou shalt say over it the following Psalms: CXXXIII, CXVII. (133 & 117)."

ANAIRETON

Symbol for the Silken Cloth

אדני:אמתיה : אנאירטון:
פרימומתון:אגלא:אין סיף:
קדיש:שמהמפורש:

"When any Instrument of the Art is properly consecrated, it should be wrapped in silk and put away, as we have said.

"Take, then, silk of any colour except black or grey, whereon write the words and Characters...

"Perfume it with incense of good odour, sprinkle it, and recite Psalms LXXXII.; LXXII.; CXXXIV.; LXIV. (82,72,134,64)

"After this thou shalt put it aside for seven days with sweet spices and thou shalt use this silk to wrap all the Instruments of the Art."

ENGLISH TRANSLATION OF HEBREW NAMES

אדני:אמתיה : אנאירטון:
פרימומתון:אגלא:אין סיף:
קדיש:שמהמפורש :

ANAIRETON : EMETEH (Truth?) : ADONAI
AIN SOPH : AGLA : PRIMUMATON
SHEMHAMPHORESH : QADOSH

THE SPRINKLER

Symbols For The Front

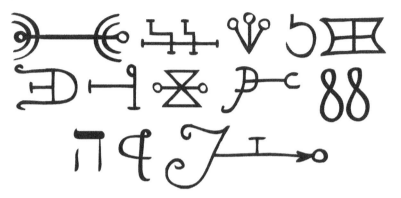

Symbols For The Back

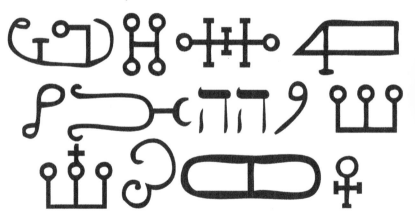

"If it be necessary to sprinkle with water anything required in the art it should be done with a sprinkler. Prepare a censer in the day and hour of Mercury, with the odoriferous spices of the art. After this thou shalt take a vessel of brass, of lead varnished within and without, or of earth, which thou shalt fill with most clear spring water, and though shalt have salt, and say these words over the salt:

"*TZABAOTH, MESSIACH, MANUEL, ELOHIM, GIBOR, YOD HE VAU HE; O God who art the truth and the life, deign to bless and sanctify this creature of salt to serve unto us for help, protection and assistance in this art, experiment and operation, and may it be a succour unto us.*

"*After this cast salt into the vessel wherein is the water, and say the following Psalms CII, LIV, VI, LXVII. (102, 54, 6, 67)*

"*Thou shalt then make unto thyself a sprinkler of vervain, fennel, lavender, sage, valerian, mint, garden-basil, rosemary and hyssop, gathered in the day and hour of mercury, the moon being in her increase. Bind together these herbs with a thread spun by a young maiden and engrave upon the handle on the one side the characters shown and on the other side those given...*

"*After this thou mayest use the water, using the sprinkler whenever it is necessary; and know that wheresoever thou shalt sprinkle this water, it will chase away all phantoms and they shall be unable to hinder or annoy any. With this same water thou shalt make all the preparations of the art.*"

I would recommend that the symbols be engraved or painted onto a rod of wood, like a small wand, around 8"/20cm. The herbs can then be arranged around the rod, and secured with the thread, creating what is in effect a small broom.

The Herbs:

The herbs used in the creation of the sprinkler are all relatively easy to grow yourself or obtain through a third party. I would recommend using fresh herbs and gathering them as near to the required date as possible so they don't lose their strength and vibrancy.

Vervain: *Verbena Officinalis*
Fennel: *Foeniculum Vulgare*
Lavender: *Lavadnula Angustifolia*
Sage: *Salvia Officinalis*
Mint: *Mentha Sachalinensis*
Garden-Basil: *Ocimum Basilicum*
Rosemary: *Rosmarinus Officinalis*
Hyssop: *Hyssopus Officinalis*

The Pen

"All things employed for writing etc., in this art should be prepared in the following manner.

"Thou shalt take a male gosling, from which thou shalt pluck the third feather of the right wing, and in plucking it thou shalt say:

"ADRAI, HAHLII, TAMAH, TILONAS, ATHAMAS, ZIANOR, ADONAI, Banish from this pen all deceit and error, so that it may be of virtue and efficacy to write all that I desire. Amen

"After this thou shalt sharpen it with the penknife of the art, perfume it, sprinkle it, and place it aside in a silken cloth."

The Reed Knife

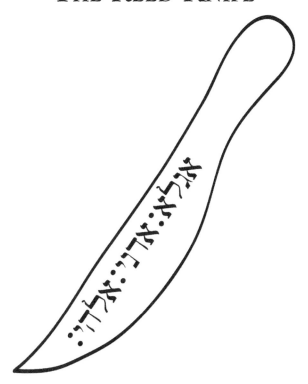

"Thou shalt have a marsh-reed cut at a single stroke with a new knife, and thou shalt strip from it the leaves, repeating this Conjuration:

THE CONJURATION OF THE REED:

"I conjure thee by the Creator of all things, and by the King of Angels, Whose Name is EL SHADDAI, that thou receivest strength and virtue to flay this animal nd to construct the parchment whereon I may write the Holy Names of God, and hat it may acquire so great virtue that all which I shall write or do may obtain its ffect, through Him who liveth unto the Eternal Ages. Amen.

"Before cutting the Reed recite Psalm LXXII. (72)

"After this, with the Knife of the Art, thou shalt fashion the Reed into the shape f a Knife, and upon it thou shalt write these Names: AGLA, ADONAI, ELOHI, hrough Whom be the work of this Knife accomplished. Then thou shalt say:

"O God, Who drewest Moses, Thy well beloved and Thine elect, from among he Reeds on the marshy banks of the Nile, and from the Waters, he being yet but a hild, grant unto me through Thy great mercy and compassion that this Reed may eceive Power and Virtue to effect that which I desire through Thy Holy Name and he Names of Thy Holy Angels. Amen.

"This being done, thou shalt commence with this Knife to flay the Animal, hether it be Virgin or Unborn, saying:

"ZOHAR, ZIO, TALMAÏ, ADONAI, SHADDAI, TETRAGRAMMATON, nd ye Holy Angels of God; be present, and grant power and virtue unto this archment, and may it be consecrated by you, so that all things which I shall write hereon shall obtain their effect. Amen.

"The Animal being flayed, take Salt, and say thus over it:

"God of Gods, and Lord of Lords, Who hast created all things from Negative xistence, deign to bless and sanctify this Salt, so that in placing it upon this archment which I wish to make, it may have such virtue that whatsoever I may rite on it hereafter may attain its desired end. Amen.

"Afterwards rub the said parchment with the exorcised salt, and leave it in the un, to imbibe this salt for the space of an entire day. Then take a large earthen essel glazed within and without, round the outside of which thou shalt write the haracters in Figure 88. [See page 30.]

"After this thou shalt put powdered lime into the vessel, saying:

"OROII, ZARON, ZAINON, ZEVARON, ZAHIPHIL, ELION, be ye resent and bless this work so that it may attain the desired effect, through the King f the Heavens, and the God of the Angels. Amen.

"*Take then exorcised Water and pour it upon the said lime, and place the ski* *therein for three days, after which thou shalt take it thence, and scrape therefror* *the lime and flesh adhering, with the Knife of Reed.*

"*After this thou shalt cut, with a single stroke, a Wand of Hazel, long enoug* *for thee to form a Circle therewith; take also a cord spun by a young maiden, an* *small stones or pebbles from a brook, pronouncing these words:*

"*O God Adonai, Holy and Powerful Father, put virtue into these stones, tha* *they may serve to stretch this parchment, and to chase therefrom all fraud, and ma* *it obtain virtue by Thine Almighty Power.*

"*After this, having stretched the said parchment upon the Circle and bound* *with the cord and stones, thou shalt say:*

"*AGLA, YOD, HE, VAU, HE, IAH, EMANUEL, bless and preserve th* *parchment, so that no Phantasm may enter therein.*

"*Let it dry thus for three days in a dark and shady place, then cut the cord wit* *the Knife of Art, and detach the Parchment from the Circle, saying:*

"*ANTOR, ANCOR, TURLOS, BEODONOS, PHAIAR, APHARCAR, b* *present for a guard unto this Parchment.*

"*Then perfume it, and keep it in silk ready for use.*

"*No woman, if her flowers be upon her, should be permitted to see th* *parchment; otherwise it will lose its virtue. He who maketh it should be pure, clear* *and prepared.*

"*But if the preparation of the aforesaid parchment seemeth too tedious, tho* *mayest make it in the following manner, but it is not so good.*

"*Take any Parchment, and exorcise it; prepare a censer with perfumes writ* *upon the parchment the character...hold it over the incense, and say:*

"*Be ye present to aid me, and may my operation be accomplished through you* *ZAZAII, ZALMAII, DALMAII, ADONAI, ANAPHAXETON, CEDRION* *CRIPON, PRION, ANAIRETON, ELION, OCTINOMON, ZEVANION* *ALAZAION, ZIDEON, AGLA, ON, YOD HE VAU HE, ARTOR, DINOTOR* *Holy Angels of God; be present and infuse virtue into this Parchment, so that* *may obtain such power through you that all Names and Characters thereon writte* *may receive due power, and that all deceit and hindrance may depart therefrom* *through God the Lord merciful and gracious, Who liveth and reigneth through a* *the Ages. Amen.*

"*Then shalt thou recite over the parchment Psalms LXXIIl.; CXVII.; an* *CXXXIV (72, 117 and 134) and the Benedicite Omnia Opera.*

"*Then say:*

"I conjure thee, O parchment, by all the Holy Names, that thou obtainest efficacy and strength, and becomest exorcised and consecrated, so that none of the things which may be written upon thee shall be effaced from the Book of Truth. Amen.

"Then sprinkle it, and keep it as before said.

"This knife is used to flay the animal and also to remove the hair and sinew etc from the skin after it has been soaked in lime for three days. I dare say that the initial flaying would be easier if performed with a metal knife, however the scraping off of hair etc. from the lime soaked skin is ideally suited to a tool such as this, which can be made very sharp without danger of puncturing the skin."

THE VESSEL CONTAINING LIME

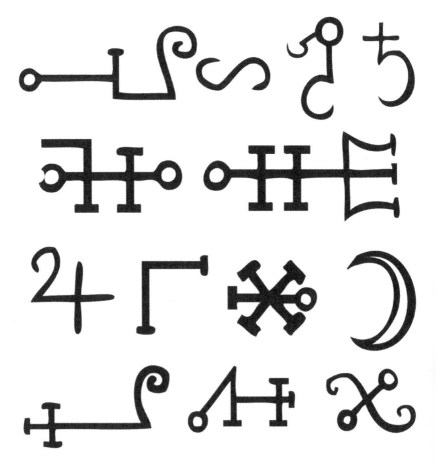

These symbols are to be placed on the outside of a glazed earthenware vessel that is to be used for the treatment of animal skin, during the process of parchment making.

THE WOODEN TRUMPET

אלהים צבאות

אלהים גבור

"First let him have a trumpet made of new wood, on the one side of which *hall* be written in Hebrew with the pen and ink of the art these names of God: *ELOHIM, GIBOR, ELOHIM, TZABAOTH;* and on the other side these *haracters.*

"Having entered in to the circle to perform the experiment, he should sound *his* trumpet towards the four quarters of the universe, first towards the east, then *owards* the south, the towards the west and lastly towards the north. Then let him *ay:*

"Hear ye, and be ye ready, in whatever part of the universe ye may be, to obey the voice of god the mighty one and the names of the creator, we let you know by this signal and sound that ye will be convoked hither, wherefore hold ye yourselves in readiness to obey our commands.

"This being one let the master complete his work, renew the circle and make the incensements and fumigations."

THE CLOTHING

THIS SECTION DETAILS THE SIGNS AND SYMBOLS TO BE EMPLOYED IN THE CREATION of the magician's vestments. There are actually very few articles needed here, and each can be made by the magician with relatively little difficulty.

The symbols need to be embroidered onto the shoes and robes using a consecrated needle, reserved especially for such purposes - the instructions for the consecration of such a needle can be found under the section regarding the sword.

THE ROBE

"*The exterior habiliments which the master of the art should wear ought to be of linen, as well as those which he weareth beneath them; and if he hath the means they should be of silk. If they be of linen the thread of which they are made should have been spun by a young maiden.*

"*The characters shown should be embroidered on the breast with the needle of art in red silk.*"

There is no indication on the "design" of the robe to be used by the magician, but taking various other grimoires into account, it's safe to assume that it should be white in colour or similar to those worn by the priesthood, or in fact an actual priestly robe, specially acquired for the purpose.

THE SHOES

"The shoes should also be white, upon which the characters should be traced in he same way (i.e. in red silk).

"The shoes or boots should be made of white leather, on which should be marked he signs and characters of art. These shoes should be made during the days of fast nd abstinence, namely, during the nine days set apart before the beginning of he operation, during which the necessary instruments also should be prepared, olished, brightened and cleaned."

THE CROWN OF THE MASTER

YOD HE VAV HE
(FRONT)

EL
(RIGHT)

ELOHIM
(LEFT)

ADONAI
(BEHIND)

"*The Master of the art should have a crown made of virgin paper, upon which should be written these four names: YOD HE VAU HE in front; ADONAI behind, EL on the right; and ELOHIM on the left. These names should be written with the ink and pen of the art, whereof we shall speak in the proper chapter...*"

There is no specific design for the paper crowns given in the *Key of Solomon*, however as they are made simply of paper, you can create as simple/complex design as your skills and personal tastes allow. From the minimal symbolism on the master's crown, a simple band of paper would most likely suffice.

The Crowns of the Disciples

LINE 1

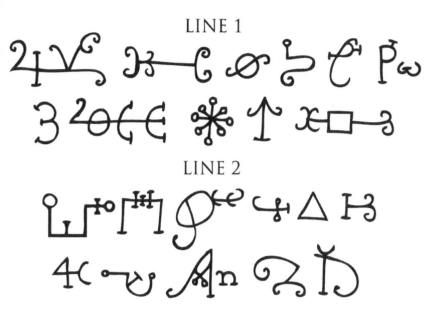

LINE 2

"...The disciples should also each have a crown of virgin paper whereon these divine symbols should be marked in scarlet."

THE WEAPONS

THE FOLLOWING TOOLS ARE ALL USED BY THE MAGICIAN IN THE CREATION OF the circle, the threatening of spirits, and also the procurement of raw materials to be used in magical operations. The uses of these items can be inferred from their design and their mundane functions; for example, the herbs used in the sprinkler are presumably cut using the sickle, the blood taken from the wing of a bat using the needle-like poniard, etc. This information is not always given in the text so it is down to the magician to use logic to marry up the tools with their appropriate uses.

I have endeavoured to give a clear illustration of each tool, as well as the accompanying text from the *Key* and an explanation of any divine and angelic names. The tools are presented in no particular order, though I would recommend that the most useful tool to create first would be the black-hilted knife as this has the most practical uses.

THE KNIFE WITH THE BLACK HILT:

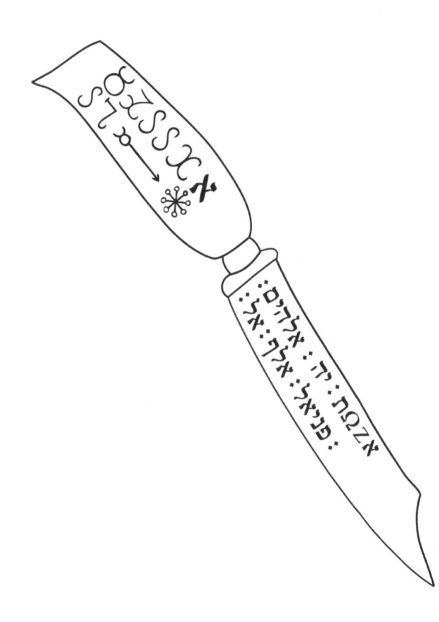

"*But as for the knife with the black hilt, for making the circle, wherewith to strike terror and fear into the spirits, it should be made in the same manner (as the knife with the white handle) except that it should be done in the day and hour of Saturn, and dipped in the blood of a black cat and in the juice of hemlock, the characters and names shown...being written thereon, from the point towards the hilt, which being completed, thou shalt wrap it in a black silk cloth.*"

This knife is one of the better known Solomonic tools, being the inspiration for the Wiccan athame and one of the easier tools for the magician to make themselves (either by buying a pre-made knife and applying the correct symbols themselves, or by having one made specifically for the purpose by a blacksmith).

In contrast to the white-handled knife, this blade is one of the tools used in the construction of the magic circle, it being used to describe the circle and divine names upon the ground.

Inscription for the Handle

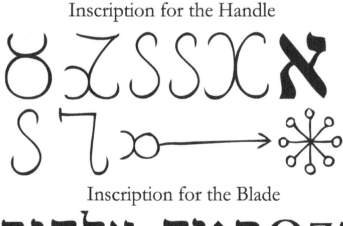

Inscription for the Blade

:אΩZת:יה:אלהים:

:פניאל:אלף:אל:

TRANSLATION OF THE BLADE:

AZOTH	אZΩת:
IAH	יה:
ELOHIM	אלהים:
EL	אל:
PENIEL	פניאל:
ALEPH	אלף:

This weapon includes the use of two lesser used words, namely Azoth and Peniel. Azoth is spelt using Latin, Greek and Hebrew letters, each letter being either the first or last of each of their respective alphabets. Azoth is an alchemical name for mercury and Peniel is mentioned in Genesis 32:30, and means Face of God.

KNIFE WITH THE WHITE HILT:

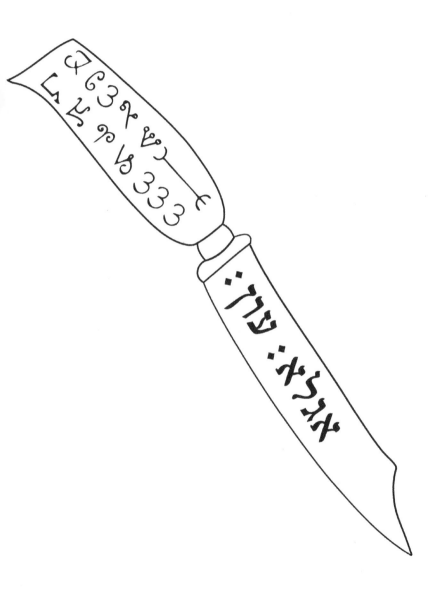

"*The knife with the white hilt should be made in the day and hour of mercury when mars is in the sign of the Ram or Scorpion. It should be dipped in the blood o a gosling and in the juice of the pimpernel, the moon being at her full or increasin in light. Dip therein also the white hilt, upon which thou shalt have engraved th characters shown, afterwards perfume it with the perfumes of art.*

"*With this knife thou mayest perform all the necessary operations of the ar except the circles. But if it seemeth unto thee too troublesome to make a simila knife, have one made in the same fashion and thou shalt place it thrice int the fire until it becometh red-hot, and each time though shalt immerse it in th aforesaid blood and juice, fasten thereunto the white hilt having engraved thereo the aforesaid characters, and upon the hilt though shalt write with the pen of ar commencing from the point and going towards the hilt, these names: AGLA, ON as shown...afterwards thou shalt perfume and sprinkle it and shalt wrap it in piece of silken cloth.*"

Inscription for the Handle

Inscription for the Blade

:אΩZת:יה:אלהים:

:פניאל:אלף:אל:

The symbols for the white-handled knife include the astrological signs for Taurus and Capricorn(?) as well as the letters Shin and Aleph rendered in the Passing The River magical alphabet.

Symbols for the Blade

עורן AIN

אגלא AGLA

THE SWORD

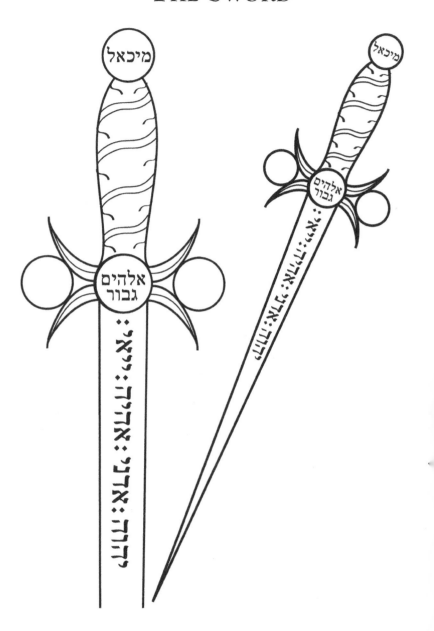

"*Swords are also frequently necessary for use in Magical Arts. Thou shalt therefore take a new Sword which thou shalt clean and polish on the day of Mercury, and at the first or the fifteenth hour, and after this thou shalt write on one side these Divine Names in Hebrew, YOD HE VAU HE, ADONAI, EHEIEH, YAYAI; and on the other side ELOHIM GIBOR; sprinkle and cense it and repeat over it the following conjuration:*"

THE CONJURATION OF THE SWORD:

"*I conjure thee, O Sword, by these Names, ABRAHACH, ABRACH, ABRACADABRA, YOD HE VAU HE, that thou serve me for a strength and defence in all Magical Operations, against all mine Enemies, visible and invisible.*

"*I conjure thee anew by the Holy and Indivisible Name of EL strong and wonderful; by the Name SHADDAI Almighty; and by these Names QADOSCH, QADOSCH, QADOSCH, ADONAI ELOHIM TZABAOTH, EMANUEL, the First and the Last, Wisdom, Way, Life, Truth, Chief, Speech, Word, Splendour, Light, Sun, Fountain, Glory, the Stone of the Wise, Virtue, Shepherd, Priest, Messiach Immortal; by these Names then, and by the other Names, I conjure thee, O Sword, that thou servest me for a Protection in all adversities. Amen.*

"*This being finished thou shalt wrap it also in silk like all the other Instruments, being duly purified and consecrated by the Ceremonies requisite for the perfection of all Magical Arts and Operations.*"

מיכאל	MICHAEL
אלהים	ELOHIM
גבור	GIBOR
הוהי	IHVH/YAHWEH
ינדא	ADONAI
היהא	EHEIEH
יאיי	YAYAI

SWORD OF THE DISCIPLES

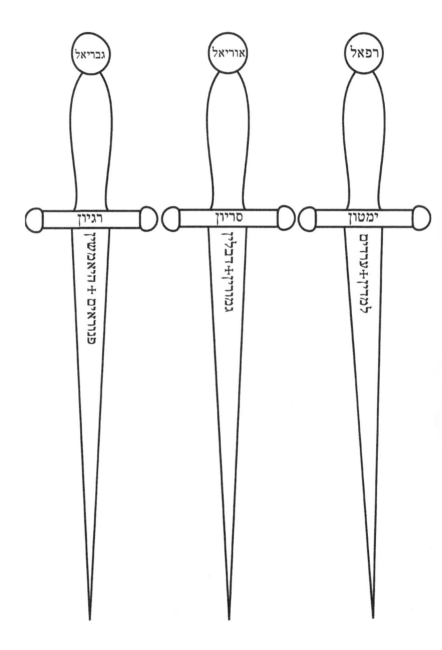

"*Three other Swords should be made for the use of the Disciples.*

"*The first one should have on the pommel the Name CARDIEL or GABRIEL on the Lamen of the Guard, REGION; on the Blade, PANORAIM HEAMESIN.*

"*The Second should have on the pommel the Name AURIEL; on the Lamen of the Guard, SARION; on the Blade, GAMORINDEBALIN.*

"*The third should have on the pommel the Name DAMIEL or RAPHAEL; on the Lamen of the Guard, YEMETON; on the Blade, LAMEDIN ERADIM.*

"*The Burin or Graver is useful for engraving or incising characters. In the day and hour either of Mars or of Venus thou shalt engrave thereon the characters shown, and having sprinkled and censed it thou shalt repeat over it the following Prayer:*"

PRAYER:

"*ASOPHIEL, ASOPHIEL, ASOPHIEL, PENTAGRAMMATON, ATHANATOS, EHEIEH ASHER EHEIEH, QADOSCH, QADOSCH, QADOSCH; O God Eternal, and my Father, bless this Instrument prepared in Thine honour, so that it may only serve for a good use and end, for Thy Glory. Amen.*

"*Having again perfumed, thou shalt put it aside for use. The Needle may be consecrated in the same way.*

"*These swords, to be carried by the disciples are "lesser" versions of the sword used by the Master, the pommels bear the names Gabriel, Raphael and Auriel, three of the four archangels, the final angel, Michael, appearing on the sword of the master.*"

NAMES ON THE DISCIPLES' SWORDS

כרדיאל גבריאל GABRIEL CARDIEL

רגיון REGION

פנוראים היאמשין PANORAIM HEAMESIN

אוריאל AURIEL

סריון SARION

גמורין דבלין GAMORIN DEBALIN

דמיאל רפאל RAPHAEL DAMIEL

ימטון YEMETON

למדין ערדים LAMEDIN ERADIM

THE STAFF AND WAND

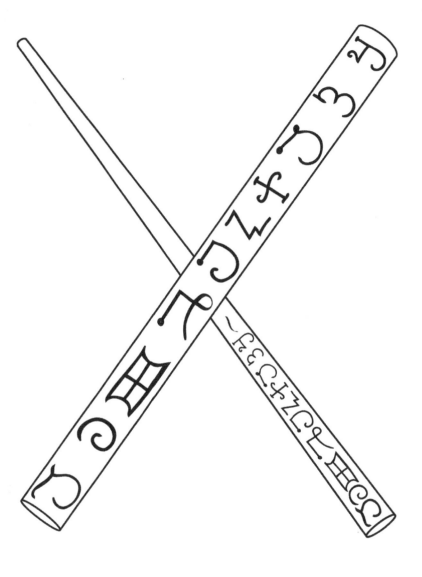

"*The Staff should be of elderwood, or cane, or rosewood; and the Wand of hazel or nut tree, in all cases the wood being virgin, that is of one year's growth only. They should each be cut from the tree at a single stroke, on the day of Mercury, at sunrise. The characters shown should be written or engraved thereon in the day and hour of Mercury.*

"*This being done, thou shalt say:*

"*ADONAI, Most Holy, deign to bless and to consecrate this Wand, and this Staff, that they may obtain the necessary virtue, through Thee, O Most Holy ADONAI, Whose kingdom endureth unto the Ages of the Ages. Amen.*

"*After having perfumed and consecrated them, put them aside in a pure and clean place for use when required.*"

Symbols for the Wand and Staff

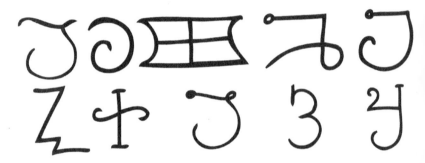

The Scimitar

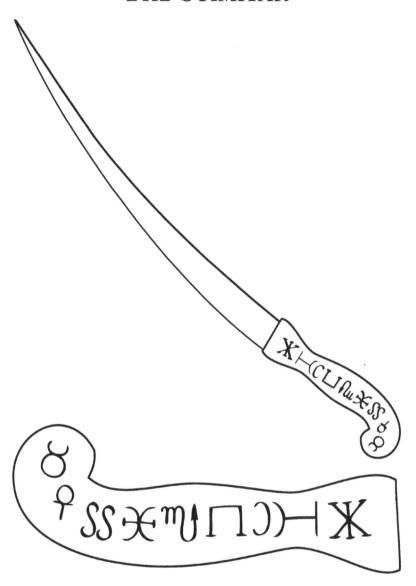

"The Scimitar...are made in the same way (as the knife with the black hilt)...in the day and hour of Mercury, and they should be dipped in the blood of a magpie and the juice of the herb Mercury. Thou must make for them handles of white boxwood cut at a single stroke from the tree, at the rising of the Sun, with a new knife, or with any other convenient instrument. The characters shown should be traced thereon. Thou shalt perfume them according to the rules of Art; and wrap them in silk cloth like the others."

Symbols for the Scimitar

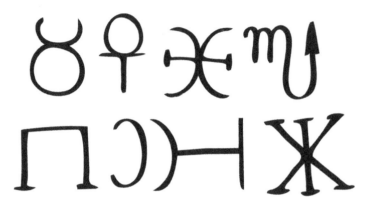

This tool and those following it share the same arrangement of 8 symbols – which include the astrological symbols for Taurus, Venus, Pisces, and Scorpio.

THE PONIARD

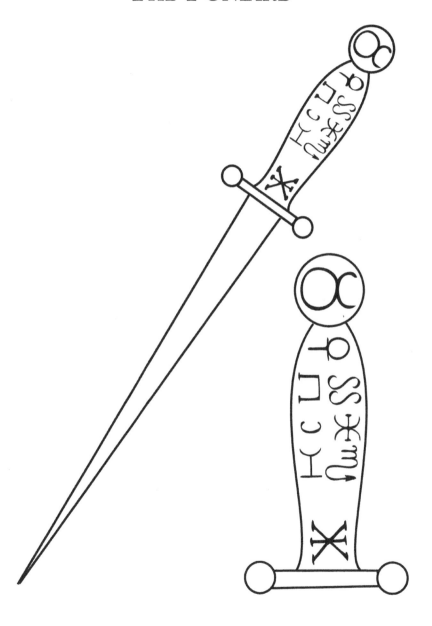

"The Poniard...are made in the same way (as the knife with the black hilt)...in the day and hour of Mercury, and they should be dipped in the blood of a magpie and the juice of the herb Mercury. Thou must make for them handles of white boxwood cut at a single stroke from the tree, at the rising of the Sun, with a new knife, or with any other convenient instrument. The characters shown should be traced thereon. Thou shalt perfume them according to the rules of Art; and wrap them in silk cloth like the others."

Poniards are a slender type of double-edged thrusting knife, popular throughout Europe during the middle ages. They are characterised by an incredibly thin triangular or square blade, terminating in an acute point. Owing to the small tip of the weapon, the Poniard may be a candidate for the tool used to extract blood from sacrificial victims, such as the magpie mentioned in this tool's construction.

THE DAGGER

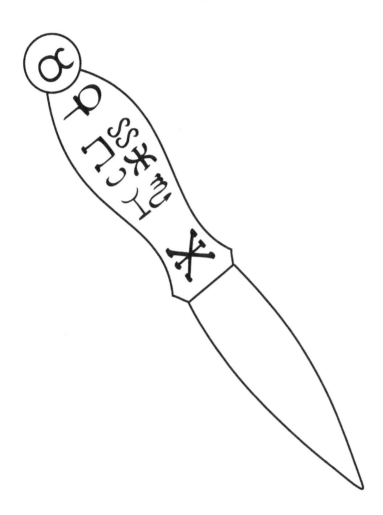

"The Dagger...are made in the same way (as the knife with the black hilt)...in the day and hour of Mercury, and they should be dipped in the blood of a magpie and the juice of the herb Mercury. Thou must make for them handles of white boxwood cut at a single stroke from the tree, at the rising of the Sun, with a new knife, or with any other convenient instrument. The characters shown should be traced thereon. Thou shalt perfume them according to the rules of Art; and wrap them in silk cloth like the others."

THE SHORT LANCE

"A short lance, wherewith to trace circles.

"The Short Lance...are made in the same way (as the knife with the black hilt)...in the day and hour of Mercury, and they should be dipped in the blood of a magpie and the juice of the herb Mercury. Thou must make for them handles of white boxwood cut at a single stroke from the tree, at the rising of the Sun, with a new knife, or with any other convenient instrument. The characters shown should be traced thereon. Thou shalt perfume them according to the rules of Art; and wrap them in silk cloth like the others."

This tool is one of the various ritual objects given with the function of drawing out circles. Previously daggers have been mentioned for this task, however a lance would not require the magician to bend down in order to make the marks on the earth.

THE SICKLE

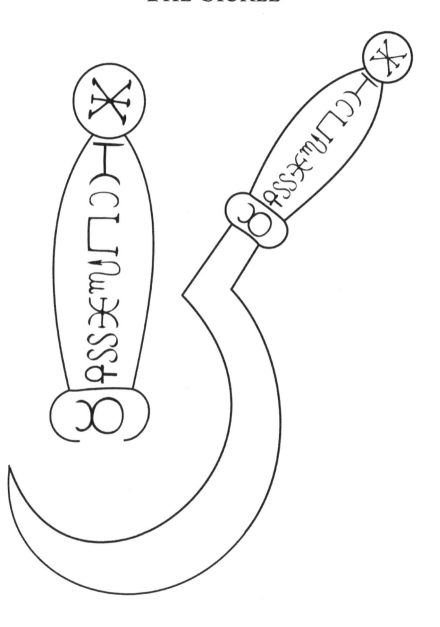

"*The Sickle...are made in the same way (as the knife with the black hilt)...in the day and hour of Mercury, and they should be dipped in the blood of a magpie and the juice of the herb Mercury. Thou must make for them handles of white boxwood cut at a single stroke from the tree, at the rising of the Sun, with a new knife, or with any other convenient instrument. The characters shown should be traced thereon. Thou shalt perfume them according to the rules of Art; and wrap them in silk cloth like the others.*"

The sickle is used as the centre point/pivot for marking out the magic circle, or to trace the circle itself. It could also be assumed that, owing to the mundane use of sickles, that this is the tool by which the magician may gather the herbs used in conjunction with the sprinkler, or other plants used in magical operations.

TOOLS FROM THE GOETIA

THE TOOLS LISTED IN THIS SECTION DO NOT APPEAR IN THE GREATER KEY OF *Solomon*, but rather in the related text *Ars Goetia (Lesser Key of Solomon)*. They are tools specifically designed for magicians who are attempting the conjuration of spirits, and on the whole offer some kind of magical protection against the 72 demons, bound by King Solomon in the Vessel of Brass. I have decided to include these illustrations here as they may be of interest to the reader.

Whereas the tools found in the *Greater Key* primarily deal with the construction of the circle within which the magician performs his experiments, the tools found in *Ars Goetia* include more task-specific tools, such as the Triangle of Art and the Vessel of Brass and, as such, it would appear that the circle building tools found in the *Greater Key* are also used in the *Lesser*.

THE PENTAGRAM OF SOLOMON

"This is the Form of Pentagram of Solomon, the figure whereof is to be made in Sol or Luna, and worn upon thy breast; having the Seal of the Spirit required upon the other side thereof. It is to preserve thee from danger, and also to command the Spirits by.

"(Colours. Circle and pentagram outlined in black. Names and Sigils within Pentagram black also. "Tetragrammaton" in red letters. Ground of centre of Pentagram, where "Soluzen" is written, green. External angles of Pentagram where "Abdia", "Ballaton," "Halliza," etc., are written, blue.)"

This well-known symbol is used during the conjuration of spirits and is best created in the form of a pendant, so that it can hang "upon thy breast" as the text indicates. It shares a protective function with the Hexagram, which is worn hanging from the magician's vestments, as we shall see shortly.

The fact that there are specific colours given for the various parts of the pentacle would suggest that apart from being cast in gold (Sol) or silver (Luna) the Pentagram can also be made from consecrated parchment, in a similar way to various other pieces of regalia.

The words around the pentagram are seemingly obscure, there is an "explanation" given at the end of the text, however there is some debate as to the usefulness of this information.

"*Soluzen. I command thee, thou Spirit of whatsoever region thou art, to come unto this circle:*

"*Halliza. And appear in human shape:*

"*Bellator (or Ballaton). And speak unto us audibly in our mother-tongue:*

"*Bellonoy (or Bellony). And show, and discover unto us all treasure that thou knowest of, or that is in thy keeping, and deliver it unto us quietly:*

"*Hallii. Hra. And answer all such questions as we may demand without any defect now at this time.*"

This does not take the name Abdia into account, and the only reference I can find to this word is that it appears to be a form of the name Obadiah, meaning "Servant of Yahweh".

Signs from the Pentagram of Solomon

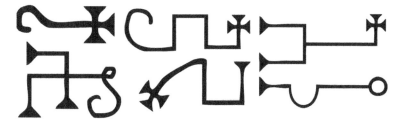

THE HEXAGRAM OF SOLOMON

"This is the Form of the Hexagram of Solomon, the figure whereof is to be made on parchment of a calf's skin, and worn at the skirt of thy white vestment, and covered with a cloth of fine linen white and pure, the which is to be shown unto the Spirits when they do appear, so that they be compelled to take human shape upon them and be obedient.

"(Colours: Circle, Hexagon, and T cross in centre outlined in black, Maltese crosses black; the five exterior triangles of the Hexagram where Te, tra, gram, ma, ton, is written, are filled in with bright yellow; the T cross in centre is red, with *the three little squares therein in black. The lower exterior triangle, where the Sigil is drawn in black, is left white. The words "Tetragrammaton" and "Tau" are in black letters; and AGLA with Alpha and Omega in red letters.)"*

Whereas the Pentagram defends the magician, the Hexagram compels the conjured spirits to interact in an intelligible way with the magician. From the description it seems that it should hang from the belt of the robe, in which case it can be fetched up into the magician's hand in order to be easily presented to attending spirits.

THE MAGIC RING OR DISK OF SOLOMON

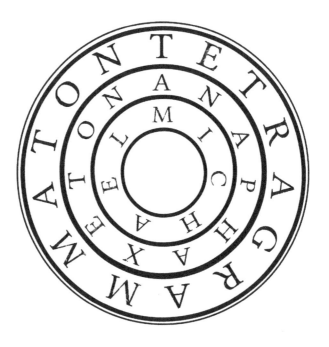

"This is the Form of the Magic Ring, or rather Disc, of Solomon, the figure whereof is to be made in gold or silver. It is to be held before the face of the exorcist to preserve him from the stinking sulphurous fumes and flaming breath of the Evil Spirits.

"(Colour, Bright yellow. Letters, black.)"

There is nothing in this short description to imply that this tool is a "ring" which is to be worn on the finger; however, many magicians have drawn this logical conclusion. The description merely states that this design should be held up to the face to prevent assault from evil spirits – attaching this disk to a ring so that it is readily available, makes the most logical sense

The names found on the disk are:

MICHAEL
ANAPHAXETON
TETRAGRAMMATON

The Magical Triangle of Solomon

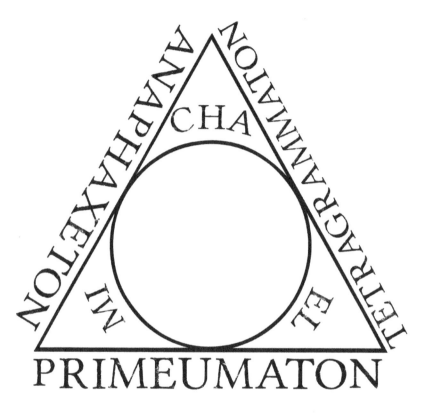

"This is the Form of the Magical Triangle, into the which Solomon did command he Evil Spirits. It is to be made at 2 feet distance from the Magical Circle and it s 3 feet across. Note that this triangle is to be placed toward that quarter where into the Spirit belongeth. And the base of the triangle is to be nearest unto the Circle, the apex pointing in the direction of the quarter of the Spirit. Observe thou also the Moon in thy working, as aforesaid, etc. Anaphaxeton is sometimes written Anepheneton.

"(Colours: Triangle outlined in black; name of Michael black on white ground; he three Names without the triangle written in red; circle in centre entirely filled n with dark green.)"

The names which surround this conjuration triangle are:

MICHAEL
TETRAGRAMMATON
PRIMEUMATON
ANAPHAXETON

This instantly recognisable diagram is somewhat synonymous with Solomonic evocation. Whilst the initial text implies that this is the focus for physical manifestation (which it certainly seems to be) it is also the place where a modern magician may wish to place a black mirror or crystal sphere in which they may perceive the non-physical body of spirit they have conjured.

THE SECRET SEAL OF SOLOMON

"This is the Form of the Secret Seal of Solomon, wherewith he did bind and seal up the aforesaid Spirits with their legions in the Vessel of Brass.

"This seal is to be made by one that is clean both inwardly and outwardly, and that hath not defiled himself by any woman in the space of a month, but hath in prayer and fasting desired of God to forgive him all his sins, etc.

"It is to be made on the day of Mars or Saturn (Tuesday or Saturday) at night at 12 o'clock, and written upon virgin parchment with the blood of a black cock that never trode hen. Note that on this night the moon must be increasing in light i.e., going from new to full) and in the Zodiacal Sign of Virgo. And when the seal is so made thou shalt perfume it with alum, raisins dried in the sun, dates, cedar and lignum aloes.

"Also, by this seal King Solomon did command all the aforesaid Spirits in the Vessel of Brass, and did seal it up with this same seal. He by it gained the love of all manner of persons, and overcame in battle, for neither weapons, nor fire, nor water could hurt him. And this privy seal was made to cover the vessel at the top withal, etc."

Symbols from the Secret Seal of Solomon

Mathers' notes suggest that the central part of this seal is a hieroglyphic representation of a man raising his arms; however, I would suggest, owing to the nature and function of this seal, that it is in fact a stylized representation of a lock, which has been barred, or crossed out.

The Magic Circle

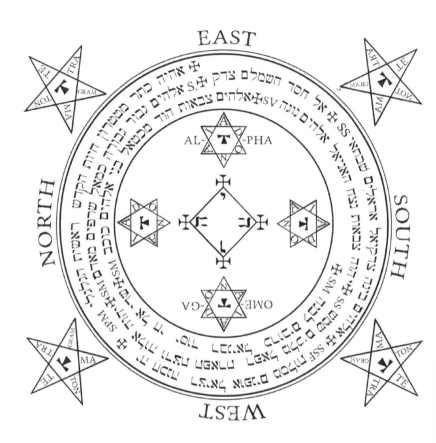

"This is the Form of the Magical Circle of King Solomon, the which he made
that he might preserve himself therein from the malice of these Evil Spirits. This
Magical Circle is to be made 9 feet across, and the Divine Names are to be written
around it, beginning at EHYEH, and ending at LEVANAH, Luna.

"(Colours: The space between the outer and inner circles, where the serpent is
coiled, with the Hebrew names written along his body, is bright deep yellow. The
square in the centre of the circle, where the word "Master" is written, is filled in
with red. All names and letters are in black. In the Hexagrams the outer triangles
where the letters A, D, O, N, A, I, appear are filled in with bright yellow, the

centres, where the T-shaped crosses are, blue or green. In the Pentagrams outside the circle, the outer triangles where "Te, tra, gram, ma, ton," is written, are filled in bright yellow, and the centres with the T crosses written therein are red.)"

The external pentagrams
(where the candles are placed)

The Internal Hexagrams

Central Square for the Magician

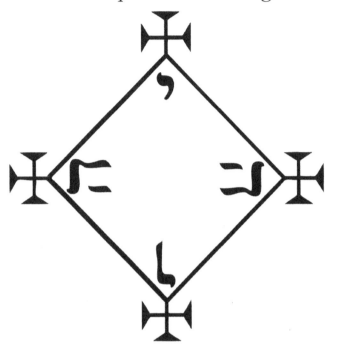

The Names Around the Circle
In English and Hebrew

חיות מטטרון כתר אהיה

EHYEH KETHER METATRON CHAIOTH

ה גלגלים ראשית ה קדש

HA-QADESH RASHITH HA-GALGALIM S.P.M.

מסלות אופנים רציאל חכמה יה

IAH CHOKMAH RATZIEL AUPHANIM MASLOTH
S.S.F

אראלים צדקיאל בינה אלהי יהוה

IEHOVAH EOLHIM, BINAH TZADQUIEL   ARALIM

יאתבש

SHABBATHAI S. OF SATURN

צדק חשמלם צדקיאל אל חסד

EL CHESED TZADQIEL CHASCHMALIM TZEDEQ
S. OF JUPITER

שרפים כמאל גבורה אלהים גבור

ELOHIM GIBOR GEBURAH KAMAEL SERAPHIM

מאדם

MADIM S. OF MARS

יהוה   אלוהודעת   תפארת

Iehovah Eloah Va-Daäth Tiphereth

שמש   מלכים   רפאל

Raphael Malakim Shemesh S. of the Sun

יהוה   צבאות   נצח   האניאל   אלהים

Iehovah Tzabaoth Netzach Haniel Elohim

נוגה

Nogah S. of Venus

אלהים   צבאות   הוד   מכטאל   אלהים   בני

Elohim Tzabaoth Hod Michael Beni Elohim

כוכב

Kokav S. of Mercury

חי   אל   שדי   יסוד   גאביאל   כרובים

Shaddai El Chai Iesod Gabriel Cherubim

לבנה

Levanah S. of the Moon.

THE VESSEL OF BRASS

"*This is the Form of the Vessel of Brass wherein King Solomon did shut up the Evil Spirits, etc. Somewhat different forms are given in the various codices. The seal...(i.e the Secret seal) was made in brass to cover this vessel with at the top. This history of the genii shut up in the brazen vessel by King Solomon recalls the story of "The Fisherman and the Jinni" in "The Arabian Nights." In this tale, however, there was only one jinni shut up in a vessel of yellow brass which was covered at the top with a leaden seal. This jinni tells the fisherman that his name is Sakhr, or Sacar.*

(Colour: Bronze. Letters: Black on a red band.)"

There are no specific instructions for the use of this vessel in the text; however, once the spirit has been conjured and is bound by the various invocations and divine names, it should be quite possible for the magician, endowed with divine authority, to command the spirits he has invoked into the vessel. It may also be possible for the resourceful magician to utilise this vessel outside of the conjuration context to help remove unwanted spirits from houses and buildings.

The central band shown in the diagrams is where the divine names are written, which are detailed on page 79. The order of the names are somewhat confused in the original diagram, however, and the logic behind the repetition of the angelic name Tzadqiel escapes me.

Divine and Angelic Names from
the Brazen Vessel

הָאַנִיאֵל: אַרָארִיתָא: הַשְׁמַלִּים:

HASHMALIM   ARARITA   HANIEL

אַשֶׁר אֶהְיֶה: גַבְרִיאֵל: מִיכָאֵל:

MICHAEL   GABRIEL   ASHER EHEH

רְפָאֵל: אַרָארִיתָא׳ צַדְקִיאֵל:

TZADQIEL   ARARITA   RAPHAEL

צַדְקִיאֵל: צַדְקִיאֵל: אֵל:

TZADQIEL   TZADQIEL   EL

כָּמָאֵל:

KAMAEL

CATALOGUE OF SYMBOLS

THE FOLLOWING PAGES CONTAIN A COMPLETE LIST OF ALL THE SYMBOLS AND sigils found on the tools of the Greater and Lesser Keys, along with their location, suggested meanings, and if they occur in other texts.

Many of the symbols seem to be abstract, their origins obscure, whereas others are more obvious in their design, being clearly based on planetary, astrological, or numerical symbols. Where possible, I have offered my opinion on what these symbols may represent; however owing to the incredibly abstract nature of so many of these symbols, that is not always possible.

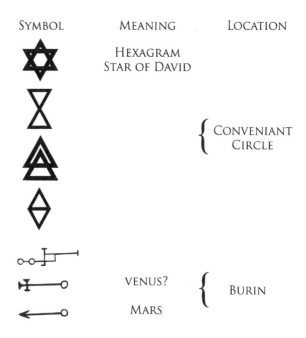

SYMBOL	MEANING	LOCATION
	HEXAGRAM STAR OF DAVID	
		CONVENIANT CIRCLE
	VENUS?	BURIN
	MARS	

	ALGOL VARIANT?	CANDLES
		CANDLES
		CANDLES
		CANDLES
		SPRINKLER CANDLES
	LUNAR CRESCENTS?	CANDLES
		CANDLES
		CANDLES
	PENTAGRAM	THE MAGIC CIRCLE
		{ THE SILKEN CLOTH

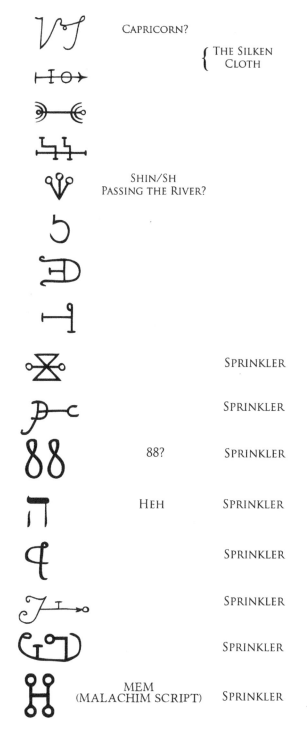

CAPRICORN?

{ THE SILKEN
  CLOTH

SHIN/SH
PASSING THE RIVER?

SPRINKLER

SPRINKLER

88?   SPRINKLER

HEH   SPRINKLER

SPRINKLER

SPRINKLER

SPRINKLER

MEM
(MALACHIM SCRIPT)   SPRINKLER

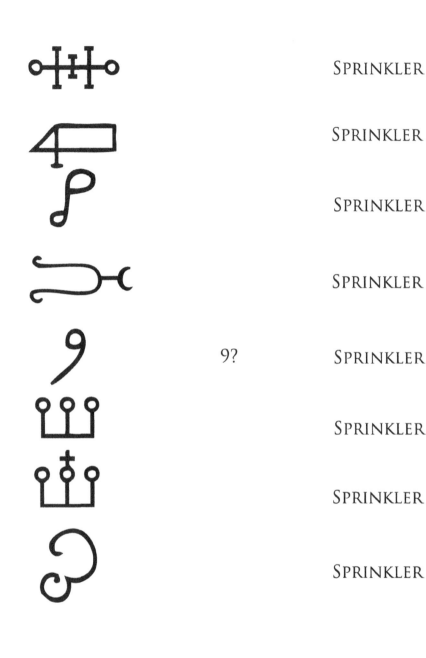

SPRINKLER

SPRINKLER

SPRINKLER

SPRINKLER

9?   SPRINKLER

SPRINKLER

SPRINKLER

SPRINKLER

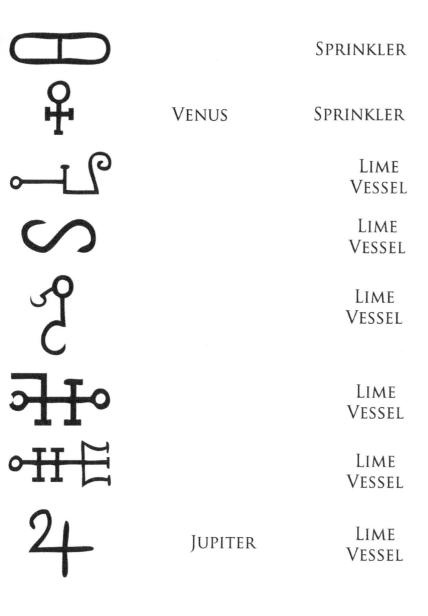

		SPRINKLER
	VENUS	SPRINKLER
		LIME VESSEL
		LIME VESSEL
		LIME VESSEL
		LIME VESSEL
		LIME VESSEL
	JUPITER	LIME VESSEL

LIME
VESSEL

LIME
VESSEL

MOON

LIME
VESSEL

LIME
VESSEL

LIME
VESSEL

STYLIZED
ALEPH?

LIME
VESSEL

	TAURUS	BLACK HILTED KNIFE
	CAPRICORN?	BLACK HILTED KNIFE
		BLACK HILTED KNIFE
	PISCES?	BLACK HILTED KNIFE
		BLACK HILTED KNIFE
	MERCURY?	BLACK HILTED KNIFE
		BLACK HILTED KNIFE

CAPRICORN   **THE WHITE HILTED KNIFE**

THE FOLLOWING SET OF SYMBOLS APPEARS ON SEVERAL OF THE WEAPONS GIVEN IN THE KEY, INCLUDING: THE PONIARD, SCIMITAR, SHORT LANCE, DAGGER AND SICKLE.

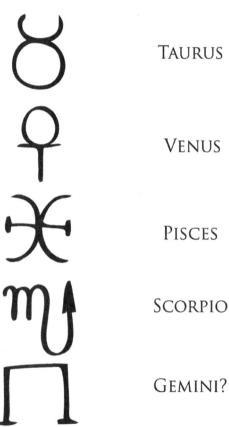

TAURUS

VENUS

PISCES

SCORPIO

GEMINI?

MOON?

SEXTILE?

(HERE ENDS THE SYMBOLS FROM THE SHARP WEAPONS)

STAFF & WAND

STAFF & WAND

STAFF & WAND

STAFF & WAND

Psalms in the
Key of Solomon

The *Greater Key of Solomon* makes use of many biblical Psalms in the creation and consecrations of the tools found therein. Below is a list of all the psalms found within in the text with their first line in English and Latin, to aid in identification. Considering the age of the text, it is most likely that the psalms have been taken from the Latin Vulgate, so the numbering found in this version of the Bible has been used.

Psalm	Opening Line

3   Psalmus David, Cum fugeret a facie Absalom filii sui.
A Psalm of David. When he fled from the face of his son, Absalom.

6   In finem in carminibus, Psalmus David, pro octava.
In parts according to verses. A Psalm of David. For the octave.

9   In finem, pro occultis filii, Psalmus David.
Unto the end. For the secrets of the Son. A Psalm of David.

31   Ipsi David intellectus. Beati, quorum remissæ sunt iniquitates: et quorum tecta sunt peccata.
The understanding of David himself. Blessed are they whose iniquities have been forgiven and whose sins have been covered.

42   Psalmus David. Iudica me Deus, et discerne causam meam de gente non sancta, ab homine iniquo, et doloso erue me.
A Psalm of David. Judge me, O God, and discern my cause from that of a nation not holy; rescue me from a man unjust and deceitful.

51   In finem, Intellectus David,
Unto the end. The understanding of David.

54   In finem, In carminibus, intellectus David.
Unto the end. In verses, the understanding of David.

60   In finem, In hymnis David.
Unto the end. With hymns, of David.

64   In finem, Psalmus David, Canticum Hieremiæ, et Ezechielis populo transmigrationis, cum inciperent exire.
Unto the end. A Psalm of David. A Canticle of Jeremiah and Ezekiel to the people of the captivity, when they began to go into exile.

67   In finem, Psalmus Cantici ipsi David.
Unto the end. A Canticle Psalm of David himself.

71   Psalmus, In Salomonem.
A Psalm according to Solomon.

72   Psalmus Asaph. Quam bonus Israel Deus his, qui recto sunt corde!
A Psalm of Asaph. How good is God to Israel, to those who are uprigh in hear

74   In finem, Ne corrumpas, Psalmus Cantici Asaph.
Unto the end. May you not be corrupted. A Canticle Psalm of Asaph

82   Canticum Psalmi Asaph.
A Canticle Psalm of Asaph.

102   Ipsi David. Benedic anima mea Domino et omnia, quæ intra me sunt nomini sancto eius.
To David himself. Bless the Lord, O my soul, and bless his holy name all that is within me.

103   Ipsi David. Benedic anima mea Domino: Domine Deus meu magnificatus es vehementer. Confessionem, et decorem induisti:
To David himself. Bless the Lord, O my soul. O Lord my God, you ar exceedingly great. You have clothed yourself with confession and beauty;

107   Canticum Psalmi ipsi David.
A Canticle Psalm, of David himself.

117   Alleluia. Confitemini Domino quoniam bonus: quoniam in sæculum misericordia eius.

Alleluia. Confess to the Lord, for he is good, for his mercy is forever.

130   Canticum graduum David. Domine non est exaltatum cor meum: neque elati sunt oculi mei. Neque ambulavi in magnis: neque in mirabilibus super me.

A Canticle in steps: of David. O Lord, my heart has not been exalted, and my eyes have not been raised up. Neither have I walked in greatness, nor in wonders beyond me.

133   Canticum graduum. Ecce nunc benedicite Dominum, omnes servi Domini: Qui statis in domo Domini, in atriis domus Dei nostri,

A Canticle in steps. Behold, bless the Lord now, all you servants of the Lord, who stand in the house of the Lord, in the courts of the house of our God.

134   Alleluia. Laudate nomen Domini, laudate servi Dominum:

Alleluia. Praise the name of the Lord. You servants, praise the Lord.

151 (There is no Psalm 151, the book of psalms ends at Psalms:150. Presumably the intened text to read is Psalm 150, rather than the fictitious 151.)

Alleluia. Laudate Dominum in sanctis eius: laudate eum in firmamento virtutis eius.

Alleluia. Praise the Lord in his holy places. Praise him in the firmament of his power.

A prayer that is also required is the *Benedicite Omnia Opera*, which is also known as *The Song of Creation*. This canticle calls on all of the universe to praise and magnify the creator, invoking not only angels and the heavens to praise him, but also frost, dew and even whales! I have given the prayer in English and Latin:

Latin:

Benedicite, omnia opera Domini, Domino; laudate et superexaltate eum in saecula.

Benedicite, caeli, Domino, benedicite, angeli Domini, Domino.

Benedicite, aquae omnes, quae super caelos sunt, Domino, benedicat omnis virtutis Domino.

Benedicite, sol et luna, Domino, benedicite, stellae caeli, Domino.

Benedicite, omnis imber et ros, Domino, benedicite, omnes venti, Domino.

Benedicite, ignis et aestus, Domino, benedicite, frigus et aestus, Domino.

Benedicite, rores et pruina, Domino, benedicite, gelu et frigus, Domino.

Benedicite, glacies et nives, Domino, benedicite, noctes et dies, Domino.

Benedicite, lux et tenebrae, Domino, benedicite, fulgura et nubes, Domino.

Benedicat terra Dominum: laudet et superexaltet eum in saecula.

Benedicite, montes et colles, Domino, benedicite, universa germinantia in terra, Domino.

Benedicite, maria et flumina, Domino, benedicite, fontes, Domino.

Benedicite, cete, et omnia, quae moventur in aquis, Domino, benedicite, omnes volucres caeli, Domino.

Benedicite, omnes bestiae et pecora, Domino, benedicite, filii hominum, Domino.

Benedic, Israel, Domino, laudate et superexaltate eum in saecula.

Benedicite, sacerdotes Domini, Domino, benedicite, servi Domini, Domino.

Benedicite, spiritus et animae iustorum, Domino, benedicite, sancti et humiles corde, Domino.

Benedicite, Anania, Azaria, Misael, Domino, laudate et

superexaltate eum in saecula.

Benedicamus Patrem et Filium cum Sancto Spiritu; laudemus et superexaltemus eum in saecula.

Benedictus es in firmamento caeli et laudabilis et gloriosus in saecula.

Amen.

ENGLISH:

O all ye Works of the Lord, bless ye the Lord : praise him, and magnify him for ever.

O ye Angels of the Lord, bless ye the Lord : praise him, and magnify him for ever.

O ye Heavens, bless ye the Lord : praise him, and magnify him for ever.

O ye Waters that be above the Firmament, bless ye the Lord : praise him, and magnify him for ever.

O all ye Powers of the Lord, bless ye the Lord : praise him, and magnify him for ever.

O ye Sun and Moon, bless ye the Lord : praise him, and magnify him for ever.

O ye Stars of Heaven, bless ye the Lord : praise him, and magnify him for ever.

O ye Showers and Dew, bless ye the Lord : praise him, and magnify him for ever.

O ye Winds of God, bless ye the Lord : praise him, and magnify him for ever.

O ye Fire and Heat, bless ye the Lord : praise him, and magnify him for ever.

O ye Winter and Summer, bless ye the Lord : praise him, and magnify him for ever.

O ye Dews and Frosts, bless ye the Lord : praise him, and magnify him for ever.

O ye Frost and Cold, bless ye the Lord : praise him, and magnify him for ever.

O ye Ice and Snow, bless ye the Lord : praise him, and magnify him for ever.

O ye Nights and Days, bless ye the Lord : praise him, and magnify him for ever.

O ye Light and Darkness, bless ye the Lord : praise him, and magnify him for ever.

O ye Lightnings and Clouds, bless ye the Lord : praise him, and magnify him for ever.

O let the Earth bless the Lord : yea, let it praise him, and magnify him for ever.

O ye Mountains and Hills, bless ye the Lord : praise him, and magnify him for ever.

O all ye Green Things upon the Earth, bless ye the Lord : praise him, and magnify him for ever.

O ye Wells, bless ye the Lord : praise him, and magnify him for ever.

O ye Seas and Floods, bless ye the Lord : praise him, and magnify him for ever.

O ye Whales, and all that move in the Waters, bless ye the Lord : praise him, and magnify him for ever.

O all ye Fowls of the Air, bless ye the Lord : praise him, and magnify him for ever.

O all ye Beasts and Cattle, bless ye the Lord : praise him, and magnify him for ever.

O ye Children of Men, bless ye the Lord : praise him, and magnify him for ever.

O let Israel bless the Lord : praise him, and magnify him for ever.

O ye Priests of the Lord, bless ye the Lord : praise him, and magnify him for ever.

O ye Servants of the Lord, bless ye the Lord : praise him, and magnify him for ever.

O ye Spirits and Souls of the Righteous, bless ye the Lord : praise him, and magnify him for ever.

O ye holy and humble Men of heart, bless ye the Lord : praise him, and magnify him for ever.

O Ananias, Azarias and Misael, bless ye the Lord : praise him, and magnify him for ever.

Lightning Source UK Ltd.
Milton Keynes UK
UKOW07f0606220515

252101UK00010B/31/P